THE HIDDEN COST OF POOR BRANDING

In Health & Wellness Practices

Alice Pettey, MFA

The Hidden Cost of Poor Branding In Health & Wellness Practices

First published 2025. NDS Enterprises LLC. Midlothian, VA.

Library of Congress Control Number: 2025900641

Paperback ISBN: 979-8-9885201-4-6

ePub ISBN: 979-8-9885201-5-3

DISCLAIMER AND/OR LEGAL NOTICES

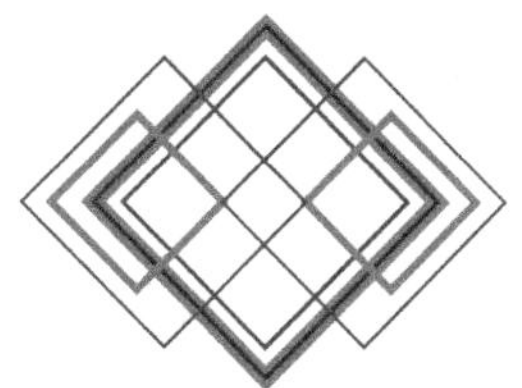

Table of Contents

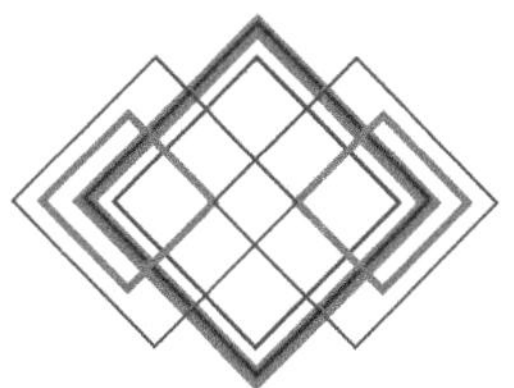

Feeling Overwhelmed? Discover How Branding Can Bring Clarity and Focus to Your Practice

Your Practice's Secret Weapon
BUILDING A BRAND THAT DRIVES SUCCESS

In today's competitive health and wellness landscape, standing out is more than just a goal—it's a necessity. That's where branding comes in. At its core, branding isn't just about a logo or a tagline; it's about creating a clear and cohesive identity that resonates deeply with your patients and staff alike. But why is branding so critical, and what can it do for your practice?

The Importance of Branding

Branding is far more than making things look pretty—it is about creating a framework and structure that serves as the backbone of your practice. This framework enables clarity, consistency, and strategic alignment across your operations. By defining and reinforcing your mission and values, branding creates a solid foundation that informs decision-making and enhances operational efficiency. The structure that guides your practice ensures every action aligns with your long-term vision. In an industry where trust, reliability, and compassionate care are paramount, a strong brand helps communicate your expertise and commitment to patient care, setting your practice apart in a crowded marketplace.

Branding serves as the foundation of your practice's identity, uniquely addressing the challenges health and wellness providers face. A solid brand image distinguishes you from the competition and deepens your connection with your community. You're building trust with new patients and improving relationships with existing ones. So how do you do it? By aligning your mission and values with your patient's expectations. A brand can help you sustain growth and have a lasting impact in this challenging environment. It communicates who you are, what you stand for, and how you deliver value. A well-crafted brand doesn't just attract patients; it builds trust and loyalty. When your brand reflects your practice's values and mission, it connects you with the right audience—those who genuinely need and appreciate your care.

For example, consider a practice specializing in family care. A brand emphasizing warmth, trust, and community will naturally resonate with parents seeking a reliable partner in their family's health journey. On the other hand, a high-tech, cutting-edge practice can attract tech-savvy individuals by showcasing innovation and expertise.

How Branding Creates Clarity and Focus

When your brand is clearly defined, it eliminates ambiguity. This clarity helps you make confident decisions about every aspect of your practice, from your services to how you engage with patients. Branding acts as a compass, providing a structured framework that guides decision-making and ensures consistency in aligning all actions and communications within your overarching goals and values. This framework enhances operational efficiency and reinforces strategic alignment, creating a cohesive vision for your practice.

This focus benefits your patients and impacts your team. When everyone in your practice understands and embodies your brand, it creates a unified approach to patient care and business operations. For instance, if your brand promises personalized care, your team will prioritize tailored interactions, making every patient feel valued and understood

Creating a Strong Internal Brand for a Thriving Practice

A **clear brand strategy** provides structure and consistency to your practice. It streamlines processes, enhances communication, and ensures uniformity across all touchpoints. However, branding is more than just external visuals or messaging—it extends internally as well. A well-defined internal brand fosters an environment where creativity, collaboration, and growth can flourish. With **clarity and alignment**, practitioners rediscover their passion for their work, sparking innovation and engagement.

Imagine a **team meeting** where every idea aligns seamlessly with your brand's vision. This environment doesn't just improve productivity—it nurtures enthusiasm, trust, and collaboration. When your internal culture reflects your brand's mission, it drives your practice forward with a sense of shared purpose.

Internal Branding in Healthcare: A Case Study on Nurse Practitioners

One of the most pressing issues in healthcare today is the **transition of Registered Nurses (RNs) to Nurse Practitioners (NPs)**. NPs play a vital role in **clinics, physician offices, and emergency care units**, increasing patient access to care, reducing physician burnout, managing chronic disease, streamlining workflows, and enhancing continuity of care. In many states, they can even practice independently without physician oversight. However, despite their value, many NPs face **barriers in securing employment** and **experience pay cuts** when transitioning from RN to NP roles.

LinkedIn discussions and studies highlight a troubling pattern—many recent NP graduates are expected to accept lower salaries than they earned as RNs, even though they take on **greater responsibilities.** This is due to a **misconception of inexperience** despite the fact that most NPs have extensive patient care experience as RNs. A study on NP employment during the COVID-19 pandemic found that many faced **a challenging job market with limited opportunities and reduced benefits**, forcing them to **accept suboptimal positions or lower pay** *(source: PMC Study).*

This **undervaluation of experience** creates frustration and disillusionment, discouraging RNs from pursuing career advancement. When organizations fail to recognize the true value of **upskilled** employees, they risk creating **an internal branding disconnect**—where stated values don't match actual treatment of staff.

Brand Alignment and Employee Engagement

If your practice seeks **greater engagement and commitment from staff**, these issues should be **top of mind**. Are you **incentivizing skill improvement** and professional growth, or are you creating barriers? Are you **aligning your message with your actions**?

For example:

- Are you encouraging continuing education but failing to provide opportunities for staff to **apply their new skills**?
- Are you benefiting from their advancement **without fair compensation**?
- Do your **values on paper** match how your staff is actually treated?

When there is a **disconnect between stated values and actual workplace culture**, it breeds **resentment, discontentment, and ultimately quiet quitting**—where employees disengage and do only the bare minimum.

The Role of Internal Branding

This is where **internal branding** comes into play. While external branding influences how your **patients perceive your practice**, internal branding defines how your **staff experiences your brand every day.** It encompasses **your vision, mission, values, and purpose**—but also includes the **behaviors, recognition, workplace culture, and rituals** that shape daily interactions.

A strong internal brand ensures that **employees feel valued, engaged, and aligned** with your practice's purpose. It **fosters job satisfaction,** helping practitioners wake up each day with a renewed sense of purpose. They don't need to "put on a mask" to reflect values they don't experience themselves. Instead, they embody and extend your practice's mission naturally, leading to **better patient experiences, stronger retention, and long-term success**.

In short, branding isn't just what your patients see—it's what your employees live. Align your internal branding with your external mission, and you'll create a practice where **staff and patients thrive together.**

Bringing Back the Joy and Excitement

Health and wellness professionals often enter their field out of a genuine desire to help others. However, the grind of running a practice can sometimes override that original passion. A strong brand can help reconnect them with their purpose, bringing back the joy of treating patients again. By focusing on what matters—delivering exceptional care—your practice becomes a place of inspiration and fulfillment.

For example, a pediatric practice might use branding to highlight its fun, child-friendly atmosphere, reminding practitioners why they chose to work with children in the first place. The result? Awed sense throughout the practice. Some fantastic examples of incorporating this type of brand-specific design into your infrastructure can be seen at idskids.com

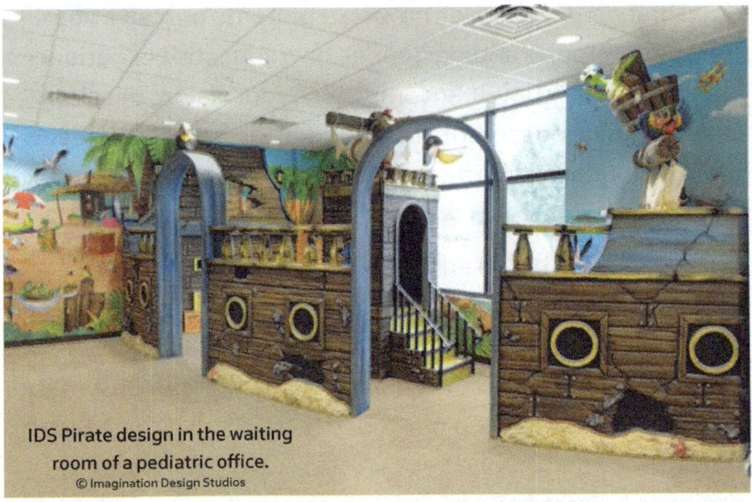

IDS Pirate design in the waiting room of a pediatric office.
© Imagination Design Studios

The Results of a Thoughtful Brand Strategy

When a brand strategy is executed effectively, the results can be transformative. Patients feel more connected and confident in your care. Staff are more engaged and aligned with the practice's mission. Your practice's reputation grows, leading to increased referrals and sustained success. A strong brand positions your practice as a provider of services and a trusted partner in health and wellness. Consider how consistent branding across your website, social media, and the scheduling experience can build trust before a patient enters the door. This alignment reassures patients they've made the right choice, leading to greater loyalty and word-of-mouth referrals.

Case Study: Virtua Health – Revitalizing a Healthcare Brand to Enhance Engagement and Trust

Problem:

Following its acquisition of Lourdes Health System, Virtua Health, South Jersey's largest health system, needed to unify its brand, enhance employee engagement, and reinforce community trust. With evolving patient expectations, the organization sought a cohesive, patient-centered identity to inspire staff and strengthen its reputation.

Solution:

Virtua Health launched a strategic rebranding initiative focused on **inclusive brand development, visual and cultural transformation, and community engagement.** Through research, including stakeholder interviews and focus groups, the organization crafted a unified message under "Here for Good," reinforcing its long-term commitment to care. The new brand featured a **lotus-inspired logo** symbolizing healing and a vibrant color palette, evoking trust and optimism. The Culture of WE initiative promoted open communication and teamwork, fostering a cohesive workplace. Additionally, Virtua Health expanded **community outreach efforts**, deepening its connection with

Virtua

Virtua
Health

local patients and residents.

Results:
The rebranding enhanced **brand recognition, workforce engagement, and community trust.** Virtua Health ranked among the **Top 50 healthcare brands nationally** and became the **highest-ranked health system in the Philadelphia and South Jersey region**. Internally, the Culture of WE improved morale, communication, and team cohesion, strengthening employee commitment to patient care. Externally, **initiatives like Chalk the Walks** increased local engagement, reinforcing Virtua Health's trusted, community-first healthcare provider role.

Virtua Health's success highlights how **a well-executed brand strategy** can transform an organization, reconnect healthcare professionals with their passion, and build lasting community trust. (*Source: Virtua Health, "Virtua Health Launches New Brand"*).

Getting Started

Whether you're building your brand from the ground up or refining an existing one, it's essential to begin with a thorough discovery process. This will help you uncover the unique strengths and opportunities that are in your practice. During this stage, you will need to identify your practice's purpose, mission, values, and goals so that you can craft a tailored brand strategy. From here, you need actionable steps that you can implement across every touchpoint of your patient's journey - both as they become patients and as you take them through your services. Please evaluate each piece to ensure that your voice and vision remain at the heart of your brand.

Investing your time and money in branding isn't just about improving the look and feel of your practice; it's about creating a framework that drives operational efficiency and strategic alignment, serving as a foundation for long-term growth and satisfaction—for—you, your team, and your patients.

Discovery Process

- ☐ Identify Purpose
- ☐ Identify Mission
- ☐ Write Out Vision
- ☐ Write Out Values
- ☐ Create 10 year goals
- ☐ Create 5 year goals
- ☐ Create 3 year goals
- ☐ Create 1 year goals
- ☐ Create quarterly goals
- ☐ Write out steps of Patients Journey
- ☐ Identify touchpoint at each step of Patients Journey
- ☐ Evaluate touchpoint for alignment with voice and vision
- ☐ Do you have standards for visual/written communications?
- ☐ Are these written down in a centralized location where all employees are able to access?
- ☐ What are your colors (codes)?
- ☐ What are your typefaces?
- ☐ What tone of voice should be used?
- ☐ Do you have a pre-selected collection of images that are approved for use?
- ☐ Are there templates for ease of consistency across the office?
- ☐ Do you understand what constitutes "on brand" or "off brand"?
- ☐ Have you explaind this to your staff?

You can uncover the true potential of your practice through the power of branding. Build a strategy that sets you apart and brings your vision to life.

Sincerely,

Alice Pettey
Founder, Certified Brand Strategist
Neurotic Dog Studios

Schedule a Free Discovery Call Today

844.621.3433

apettey@NeuroticDogStudios.com
NeuroticDogStudios.com

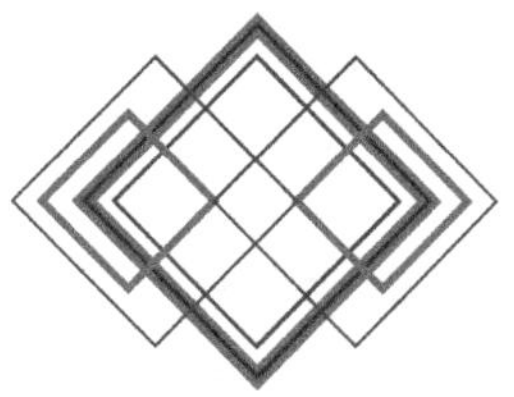

Introduction

Branding often gets pushed aside in the health and wellness field, dismissed as an afterthought or overshadowed by the pressing demands of patient care, compliance, and day-to-day operations. But your brand is so much more than a logo or tagline—it's the soul of your practice, the promise you make to every patient who walks through your door. It's how you show the world what you stand for and why you're different.

Neglecting your brand comes at a cost—a cost that may not always be obvious but is deeply felt. It's seen when a patient chooses a competitor because they didn't see the value you offer. It's felt when your staff experiences turnover because employees struggle to align with a workplace that doesn't have a clear identity. It's in the extra dollars you spend on marketing that you fail to connect with the right audience because they don't have cohesive messages or touch them emotionally. Poor branding quietly undermines your practice, chipping away at trust, loyalty, and growth.

The truth is, today's patients expect more. They aren't just looking for someone to address their immediate needs, they're searching for providers they can trust. The want, need, partners in their health journey. And long before they meet you, your brand is already doing the talking for you. What's it saying? Is it telling them about the exceptional care you provide, or is it a muddled whisper that fades into the noise of a crowded market?

This book is your guide to uncovering and addressing the hidden costs of poor branding. We'll dig into the common pitfalls, show you how to find and close branding gaps, and give you actionable strategies to build a brand that works as hard as you do. Discover how a clear, intentional brand not only attracts the right patients but also creates the environment (internal branding/culture) where your team can thrive, and your practice will grows.

Your brand tells your story. Let's make sure it's a story worth telling—a story that reflects the care, dedication, and excellence you want to deliver, and your patients deserve.

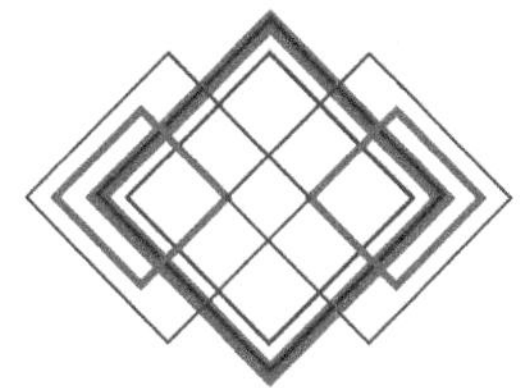

CHAPTER 1

Loss of Patient Trust and Loyalty

Trust is the foundation of every patient relationship. Unlike other industries, where transactions are often one-and-done, healthcare is deeply personal. Patients entrust you with their health, their most private concerns, and, in many cases, their physical and emotional well-being. They expect professionalism, competence, and, above all, consistency. If trust wavers, they won't just hesitate to book an appointment—they may never return.

A **strong, cohesive brand** plays a crucial role in establishing and maintaining that trust. Research shows that **75% of consumers make decisions based on visual identity**—elements such as logos, websites, and overall aesthetics *(Adobe)*. A polished, professional brand reassures patients that they're in capable hands. When branding is inconsistent or outdated, it creates doubt and uncertainty, leaving patients questioning whether the quality of care matches the quality of the brand's presentation.

When Branding Fails: Real-Life Consequences

Dr. Matthews, a chiropractor in San Diego, built his practice on

personalized care and patient loyalty, yet new patient bookings dropped by 35% over the course of a year. His care hadn't changed. His expertise hadn't diminished. The issue? His website—one of the primary ways potential patients discovered his practice—hadn't been updated in over a decade. Slow load times, an unresponsive design, and outdated information frustrated tech-savvy visitors, who abandoned the site before ever booking an appointment. That **35% drop in patient inquiries cost him an estimated $72,000 in lost revenue**.

In another case, a Denver-based wellness spa promoted itself as a **luxury experience**, promising high-end treatments and five-star service. Yet, its **marketing materials told a different story**. Instead of polished branding, the spa distributed **cheaply printed, generic flyers** around the local area. The disconnect confused potential clients—was this truly a luxury spa, or just another budget-friendly option? Disappointed customers left reviews reflecting their frustration, and the spa's **Google rating plummeted to 3.2 stars**.

These stories underscore a critical truth: **if your brand promises one experience but delivers another, patients notice—and they don't return**.

How Inconsistent Branding Undermines Trust

Brand inconsistency doesn't just create confusion—it actively damages a healthcare practice's reputation and bottom line.

Confusing Patient Expectations

Imagine walking into a clinic expecting a **calm, spa-like wellness experience**, only to find **harsh fluorescent lighting, cluttered décor, and an indifferent receptionist.** The disconnect is jarring. Patients expect seamless consistency from the moment they land on your website to the time they walk through your doors. A study in the *Journal of Patient Experience* found that **patients conceptualize their expectations in**

three domains: health outcomes, individual clinicians, and the healthcare system *(Hillen et al.)*. When branding misaligns with patient experience, **distrust grows, and loyalty declines**.

Eroding Professional Perception

Branding is **silent communication**. Patients form i**nstant impressions** based on what they see—even before their first appointment. A poorly designed **logo, outdated signage, or mismatched marketing materials** can subtly suggest **disorganization or lack of attention to detail**. A study on **healthcare branding and reputation management** emphasizes that **a strong brand identity is crucial for establishing trust and credibility** *(Jadhav & Bagul)*. If your practice looks outdated or inconsistent, **patients may assume your care is, too.**

Reducing Word-of-Mouth Referrals

Word-of-mouth is one of the **most powerful marketing tools in healthcare**. Patients **trust recommendations** from friends, family, and online reviews more than any advertisement. However, **if branding leaves patients uncertain or unimpressed, they won't recommend your practice**. Even small inconsistencies—such as **mismatched colors, typographical errors, or conflicting information**—can erode trust. A case study highlighted how a **medical practice improved its reputation and increased referrals** simply by maintaining **brand consistency across all patient communications and marketing materials** (Smith).

The Data: Why Branding Matters

Branding isn't just about aesthetics—it directly impacts **patient trust, engagement, and revenue**. Consider these findings:

- **83% of patients cite trust as the most critical factor when choosing a healthcare provider** *(PwC)*.

- **Consistent branding increases consumer trust by 33%** *(Lucidpress).*
- **Poor design can reduce patient engagement rates by as much as 50%** *(Nielsen).*

The numbers don't lie—branding directly influences **how patients perceive and engage with your practice.**

How to Rebuild Trust Through Branding

If your branding is **outdated, inconsistent, or unprofessional**, it's time to realign your message with your patient experience.

1. **Conduct a Brand Audit**
   Take an honest look at your **website, social media, signage, and marketing materials.** Identify outdated elements or inconsistencies that could undermine patient trust.

2. **Invest in Professional Design**
   Work with **brand strategists, graphic designers, and copywriters** to create polished, engaging materials that reflect your values and professionalism.

3. **Leverage Patient Testimonials**
   Highlight **real stories of patient success and satisfaction**. Testimonials and case studies reassure potential patients that you deliver on your promises.

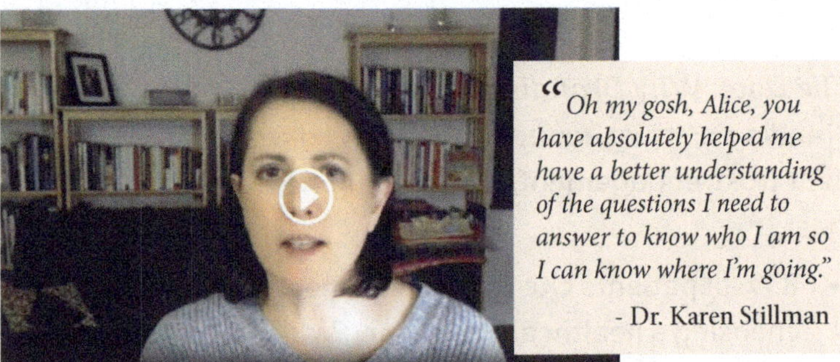

4. **Align Internal Culture with Branding**
   Train your team to **embody your brand values**. Every interaction, from **reception to treatment**, should reinforce your brand's credibility and mission.

Self-Check Quiz: Is Your Branding Building or Breaking Trust?

1. Does your website reflect the **current** quality of care you provide? (Yes/No)
2. Are all your marketing materials **consistent** in style, messaging, and quality? (Yes/No)
3. Do your **online reviews align** with the brand experience you want to convey? (Yes/No)
4. If a patient visited your website, then walked into your practice, would their experience **match their expectations**? (Yes/No)
5. Are your **staff and patient communications aligned** with your brand's promise? (Yes/No)

If you answered 'No' to any of the above, it's time to take action. Consistency is key to patient trust, and **your brand should reflect the care and expertise you bring to your practice every day.**

The Cost of Ignoring Branding Issues

Branding isn't just about looking good—it's about **creating genuine, lasting connections** with your patients. Practices that fail to maintain a strong, consistent brand face serious long-term consequences:

❌ **Decreased patient trust → Fewer new patients**

❌ **Poor branding → Negative online reviews**

❌ **Inconsistent messaging → Loss of revenue**

Investing in branding is investing in your practice's future. A **strong, authentic brand transforms patients into lifelong advocates**. It's not about **making things pretty**—it's about making things **trustworthy, recognizable, and aligned** with the exceptional care you provide.

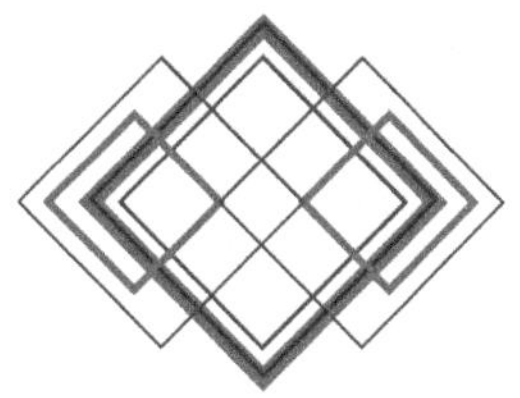

CHAPTER 2

Missed Revenue Opportunities

A strong, well-crafted brand does more than attract attention—it drives revenue. Branding is a magnet, drawing the right patients to your practice, reinforcing your credibility, and setting you apart from competitors. Without a clear, distinct brand, practices often struggle to communicate their value effectively, leaving money on the table. Poor branding results in fewer inquiries, lower retention rates, and lost patients to competitors who articulate their unique offerings more effectively.

The Financial Impact of Poor Branding

Many health and wellness practices **underestimate the link between branding and profitability**. According to Accenture, **70% of consumers are willing to pay a premium for trustworthy brands**. Without a **consistent, compelling brand identity**, practices fall into the common trap of competing solely on price. This **erodes profitability**, reduces perceived value, and makes **attracting and retaining** the right patients harder.

When branding fails to differentiate a practice, potential patients gravitate toward competitors whose **messaging is clearer and more aligned** with their needs. Patients make decisions based on **trust and confidence**, and if your brand doesn't convey these qualities, they will seek a provider that does. Over time, these **missed inquiries, low retention rates, and lack of referrals** translate into significant revenue loss.

Case Study: MedStar Health's Rebranding Success
A compelling example of branding's financial impact is **MedStar Health,** the largest not-for-profit healthcare system in Maryland and Washington, D.C. With **nine hospitals and over 130 clinics**, MedStar faced a challenge—its disjointed branding created confusion and weakened patient trust. The organization needed a **unified, recognizable identity** to enhance its credibility and streamline patient experience.

To address this, MedStar conducted an extensive **brand audit**, identifying inconsistencies and developing a master-brand strategy. Their efforts included a rapid rebranding rollout, notably converting their **entire fleet of 120 vehicles** to the new branding in just two weeks. The results were immediate: **increased brand awareness, stronger patient trust, and improved organizational cohesion** *(BrandActive)*.

This case underscores a critical takeaway: **branding isn't just about aesthetics—it's a strategic asset that drives trust, patient retention, and, ultimately, revenue growth**. Without a strong, unified brand, practices risk **losing visibility, credibility, and long-term profitability** *(BrandActive, 2023)*.

Real-Life Examples of Missed Revenue Due to Poor Branding

Generic Marketing Costs a Therapy Center New Clients
A mental health therapy center in Austin marketed itself as offering "**high-quality care**"—but so did every other clinic in the area. With no clear message that set them apart, the practice blended into the background. Patients chose competitors who

marketed their specialized services, such as **trauma-informed therapy or couples counseling**, making their offerings more relevant and appealing.

> *Financial Impact:* Despite spending heavily on advertising, the therapy center's conversion rate was **20% lower than competitors with clear branding and niche messaging**.

Chiropractor Struggles with Retention

A chiropractor's office **relied heavily on word-of-mouth referrals** but never invested in branding or patient engagement strategies. As a result, many **first-time patients didn't return,** not because of poor service but because they didn't feel **connected** to the practice or its values.

> *Revenue Loss:* The practice lost an **estimated $50,000 annually** in potential revenue due to poor retention.

How Poor Branding Limits Revenue Streams

Branding isn't just about **marketing**—it directly impacts how a practice operates and **earns.** Here's how weak branding limits revenue potential:

1. **Lack of Differentiation in a Crowded Market**
   Health and wellness practices operate in an **increasingly competitive environment**. Without branding that clearly highlights **unique strengths**, it's easy to get lost in the noise.

> *Example:* A **yoga studio** that fails to highlight its **eco-friendly ethos or community-focused approach** will struggle to stand out against larger, well-branded competitors.

2. **Fewer Referrals & Weak Word-of-Mouth Marketing**
   Patients recommend practices they feel emotionally connected to. Without a strong brand that fosters **trust and**

loyalty, patients are **less likely to refer** friends and family.

3. **Difficulty Upselling Services**
   A poorly positioned brand **limits perceived value,** making selling **premium services** like **personalized wellness plans, advanced therapies, or ongoing memberships harder**. Patients who don't associate your brand with **expertise and quality** won't see the **value in paying for premium offerings.**

Industry Data: Branding & Profitability

The numbers make it clear: **practices that invest in branding see stronger financial performance.**

📈 **33% more profitability –** Businesses that consistently invest in branding outperform those that don't *(McKinsey)*.

📈 **57% of patients are more likely to choose a practice** that effectively communicates its unique value *(PwC)*.

📈 **20% increase in patient acquisition rates –** Companies with a recognizable brand attract new patients more effectively than competitors *(Nielsen)*.

Opportunities Gained with Strong Branding

A well-crafted brand **doesn't just look good**—it unlocks **tangible revenue potential** by attracting and retaining high-value patients.

1. **Increased Conversion Rates**
   When patients **understand your brand and values,** they're more likely to book appointments and commit to ongoing care.

2. **Higher Patient Lifetime Value (PLV)**
   Loyal patients who feel **connected to your brand** are more likely to **return for follow-ups, purchase additional ser-**

vices, and refer others.

3. **Pricing Power & Reduced Price Sensitivity**
   A **strong, professional brand** allows practices to **charge premium prices** without resistance. Patients associate **strong branding with quality and expertise**, making cost a **secondary** consideration.

Actionable Steps to Capture Missed Revenue

Branding is an **investment,** not an expense. Here's how to **maximize revenue** through strategic branding:

1. **Define and Communicate Your Unique Value Proposition (UVP)**
   Identify **what sets your practice apart** and ensure this message is **woven into all marketing efforts**.

2. **Invest in Branding to Build Visibility**
   A **cohesive visual identity** that reflects your mission **builds trust** and speaks directly to your target audience.

3. **Embrace Niche Marketing**
   Position your practice **as a leader i**n a specialized area, such as **pediatric dentistry, sports therapy, or holistic nutrition.**

4. **Leverage Digital Tools**
   A **strong online presence** reinforces credibility. **SEO-optimized websites, targeted social media campaigns and email marketing** ensure you reach and engage the right audience.

The Cost of Inaction

Every patient who chooses a **competitor** or fails to return for follow-up care represents lost revenue. Over time, these **missed opportunities** compound, leaving practices struggling to **grow or sustain operations**.

Without a **cohesive brand strategy**, patient **trust weakens**, marketing **loses effectiveness**, and **competition becomes more difficult**. But with **strategic branding**, practices don't just attract new patients—they **create loyal advocates** who **return, refer others, and invest in premium services**.

Branding is not just about **aesthetics**—it's about **revenue, retention, and long-term sustainability.** Investing in a strong brand today means **securing financial growth and patient loyalty** for years.

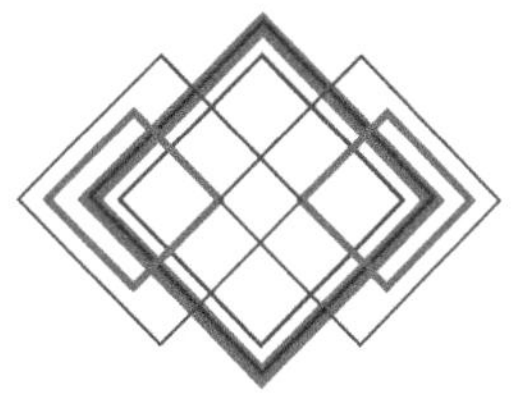

CHAPTER 3

Reduced Employee Morale and Retention

Behind every successful health and wellness practice is a **dedicated team** that brings the brand to life. Employees who feel **connected** to their organization's values and mission perform at their best, contribute to a **positive patient experience**, and foster a culture of **trust and engagement**. However, **poor branding—or the absence of a cohesive brand strategy—creates confusion, frustration, and disengagement among staff.** Over time, this leads to **low morale, high turnover, and increased recruitment costs**—all of which impact patient care and practice profitability.

What is Branding in a Healthcare Setting?

Branding goes beyond logos, color schemes, and marketing materials—it is the **identity** of a practice. In a healthcare setting, **effective branding** consists of:

- A **clear mission and values** that align with both **patient care** and **employee expectations**.
- **Consistent messaging and culture** that reinforce what the practice stands for.

- A **work environment that reflects and supports the brand's core promise**.

Defining Key Branding Concepts

- **Brand Audit:** A structured evaluation of all branding elements (website, patient materials, employee engagement strategies) to identify inconsistencies and areas for improvement.
- **Brand Values:** The **guiding principles** that shape a practice's culture, behavior, and decision-making.
- **Internal Branding:** How branding influences the employee experience, ensuring staff embody and communicate the practice's mission in patient interactions.
- When branding is **aligned** internally, employees **feel a sense of purpose**—leading to stronger engagement, higher retention, and a **better overall patient experience**.

The Connection Between Branding and Employee Engagement

Branding isn't just for patients—it's for **your team, too**. A well-defined brand serves as a compass, providing **clarity, motivation, and direction**. Employees who understand and align with a practice's mission are more **engaged, motivated, and committed** to its success. On the other hand, when branding is **unclear or inconsistent**, staff may feel **detached**, uncertain of their role, and less invested in the organization.

A **study by Gallup** found that companies with **high employee engagement** see **21% higher profitability** and **17% lower turnover** than disengaged workplaces *(Gallup, 2023)*. Internal alignment with branding **fosters pride, loyalty, and teamwork,** ensuring that staff **stay longer and perform better.**

Real-Life Examples: Branding's Impact on Employee

Morale

Case Study: A Wellness Clinic with No Clear Identity

A **Chicago-based wellness clinic** offered competitive salaries and a strong benefits package but struggled with **high turnover rates. Exit interviews revealed that employees felt disconnected from the clinic's mission** and frustrated by **inconsistent messaging.** Some were unsure whether the clinic focused on **holistic wellness, traditional medicine, or a hybrid approach**—making it difficult to **align their roles with patient expectations.**

Branding Strategy Implementation:

- ☐ Conducted a **brand audit** to assess inconsistencies in **marketing, patient education, and employee messaging.**
- ☐ Defined a **clear brand identity**, emphasizing **integrative, patient-centered care.**
- ☐ Updated **patient materials, website, and internal training programs** to reflect the new mission.
- ☐ Hosted **branding workshops** where staff contributed to defining core values.

> *Impact:* Employee satisfaction increased by **35%**, turnover rates dropped by **20%**, and the clinic saved an estimated **$150,000 annually** in recruitment and training costs *(Glassdoor, 2023).*

Case Study: Building Team Unity Through Branding

A **Seattle-based dental** practice faced **disengagement among staff and inconsistent patient experiences**. Employees lacked a clear understanding of the practice's mission, leading to **disjointed service delivery** and fluctuating patient reviews.

Branding Strategy Implementation:

- ☐ Developed **brand values** emphasizing **patient-centered care and personalized interactions**.

- ☐ Integrated **branding training modules** into **new employee onboarding and ongoing team meetings.**
- ☐ Launched an **employee recognition program**, rewarding staff who embodied the brand's mission.

> *Impact:* Employee satisfaction increased **by 35%**, turnover rates **dropped by 20%**, and patient Google reviews **improved by 1.8 stars** within a year *(LinkedIn Talent Solutions, 2023).*

How Poor Branding Erodes Employee Morale

1. **Confusion and Frustration**
   When branding is **unclear**, employees struggle to understand **what the organization stands for**—leading to a **lack of direction** in patient interactions.

   > *Example:* A **yoga studio** with no consistent messaging left **instructors unsure** of how to communicate the brand's values during classes, causing frustration and disconnection from the mission.

2. **Lack of Pride in the Workplace**
   Employees want to **feel proud** of where they work. **Poor branding makes it difficult for them to confidently represent the practice.**

   > *Example:* A **spa with outdated marketing materials** found that **front-desk staff hesitated to promote services** because the branding **didn't match the high quality of care** offered.

3. **Missed Opportunities for Team Building**
   A strong brand **unites employees around a shared mission**. Without it, teams often **operate in silos,** leading to **miscommunication and inefficiency.**

Industry Data: Branding and Employee Retention

- **69% of employees** say they would work harder if their efforts **aligned with the company mission** *(Glassdoor, 2023).*
- **Companies with strong employer branding** reduce turnover by **28%** and attract **50% more qualified candidates** *(LinkedIn, 2023).*
- **Organizations with engaged employees** outperform competitors by **147% in earnings per share** *(Gallup, 2023).*

Building Employee Engagement Through Branding

Strong branding empowers employees to **feel valued contributors** to the practice's success. By integrating branding into workplace culture, health and wellness practices can create a **more engaged, motivated, and loyal team.**

Actionable Steps for Improving Alignment:

1. **Integrate Branding into Onboarding**
   From day one, educate employees on the **practice's mission, values, and branding strategy.** Provide **examples** of how branding translates into daily roles.

2. **Incorporate Branding into Internal Communications**
   Regularly **reinforce branding values** in **team meetings, newsletters, and recognition programs.** Highlight how employees contribute to the brand's success.

3. **Empower Staff as Brand Ambassadors**
   Train employees to **consistently represent the brand** in patient interactions. Celebrate team members who reinforce the brand's mission.

4. **Foster a Sense of Ownership**
   Involve employees in **branding initiatives** like **campaign brainstorming and marketing material feedback.** When staff **feel like stakeholders**, engagement increases.

5. **Recognize and Reward Brand Alignment**
   Acknowledge employees who **exemplify the brand's values** through **patient care, teamwork, or innovative ideas.** Recognition boosts morale and reinforces desired behaviors.

Conclusion: Branding as an Internal Asset

Your brand isn't just for **patients**—it's for **your team**. A **well-defined, consistently communicated brand** fosters **alignment, pride, and motivation** among employees. By investing in branding as an **internal asset**, health and wellness practices can **reduce turnover, boost morale, and create a unified team** that delivers **exceptional patient care.**

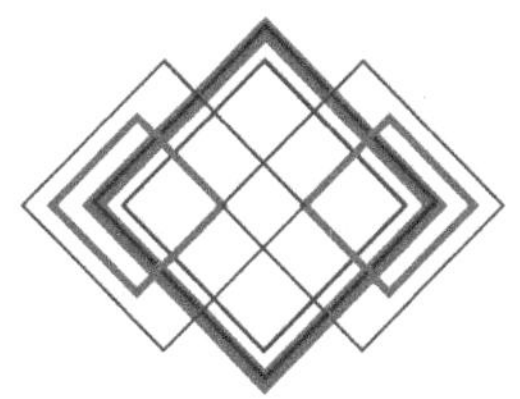

CHAPTER 4

Increased Marketing Expenses

Marketing in the **health and wellness industry** isn't just about **getting your name out there**—it's about **attracting the right patients and keeping them engaged**. However, when branding is weak or inconsistent, marketing efforts become inefficient, forcing **practices to spend more while achieving less**. Without a clear brand identity, every new campaign starts from scratch, leading to **higher costs, lower engagement, and diminishing returns on investment (ROI).**

A **study by Lucidpress** found that businesses with **consistent branding across all platforms see a 33% increase in marketing ROI**. Yet, many health and wellness practices operate with **disjointed branding**, leading to **campaigns that fail to connect, rising ad costs, and an endless cycle of redesigns and rebranding** *(Lucidpress, 2023)*.

The Financial Drain of Disconnected Marketing

Think of branding as a **compass** for your marketing. When it's clear and **consistent**, marketing efforts **build momentum,** reinforcing a recognizable message across platforms. But when branding is **inconsistent or undefined**, marketing becomes a

series of costly missteps—a never-ending effort to redefine messaging, visuals, and tone.

To put it in perspective, **companies with a cohesive brand experience see up to 4x more visibility across platforms** *(Nielsen, 2023)*. In contrast, practices without a strong brand presence **spend more on advertising just to stay visible**, often with fewer results.

Case Study: The Scattershot Approach
A **physical therapy clinic in Denver** wanted to attract more patients, so it launched **multiple marketing campaigns**—digital ads, billboards, and direct mailers. However, there was a **problem**:

- Each campaign used **different colors, fonts, and taglines**, making it difficult for potential patients to **recognize the brand.**
- Some ads focused on **sports recovery**, while others highlighted **general pain relief, leading to mixed messaging.**
- There was **no consistency** between the clinic's website, social media, and in-office branding.

> *Financial Impact:* Despite spending **$25,000 on marketing in six months**, patient inquiries barely increased. Compared to competitors with **cohesive branding**, the clinic's **cost per lead was double**.
>
> *Key Takeaway:* Without a **consistent visual identity and messaging**, marketing efforts **become diluted**, requiring **more spending to achieve minimal results**.

How Poor Branding Increases Marketing Expenses

1. **Ineffective Campaigns**
   Marketing without a **strong brand identity** results in **vague or uninspiring campaigns** that fail to stand out.

> *Example:* A wellness spa promoting "relaxation services" struggled to differentiate itself from competitors. Patients had no compelling reason to choose them over another spa that had **a clear brand promise of holistic healing through organic treatments.**

2. **Frequent Rebranding & Redesigns**
   Practices with **inconsistent branding** often feel the need to refresh their image, leading to repeated design, printing, and promotional costs.

> *Example:* A **chiropractic clinic changed its logo three times in five years,** spending over **$20,000 on rebranding efforts alone.** Instead of refining its **core brand message**, it relied on **visual updates**, which did little to improve patient engagement.

3. **Higher Ad Spend to Compensate for Weak Messaging**
   Without a **clear value proposition**, ads **require more spending to generate the same level of engagement**.

> *Example:* An **urgent care center** ran Facebook and Google ads to **increase patient bookings**. However, since **each ad had a different message and design**, patients didn't **immediately recognize the brand**—forcing the clinic to **spend 35% more on retargeting ads** just to reinforce awareness.

4. **Lost Opportunities Due to Lack of Brand Recognition**
   Consistent branding **builds recall**—patients recognize your logo, tagline, and message **instantly**. Without it, practices have to **constantly reintroduce themselves**.

> *Example:* A **nutritionist who frequently changed her website design and messaging** found that even **loyal clients struggled to refer her**—they couldn't confidently describe her brand or services.

Industry Data: The ROI of Strong Branding

The numbers **paint a clear picture**: branding **drastically** affects marketing efficiency and profitability.

- 📊 **Brands with consistent visuals and messaging** across all marketing channels see a 23% increase in revenue *(Forbes, 2023).*
- 📊 **Poorly branded campaigns generate 50% fewer clicks and conversions** than campaigns with a **clear brand identity** *(HubSpot, 2023).*
- 📊 **Companies with a cohesive brand experience see up to 4x more visibility** across platforms *(Nielsen, 2023).*

What does this mean? Strong branding doesn't just **enhance reputation**—it **reduces marketing costs, improves engagement, and drives revenue growth.**

Opportunities to Reduce Marketing Costs Through Branding

Strong branding allows **every marketing dollar to go further.** By building a **recognizable identity**, practices can **focus on high-impact strategies** rather than relying on **high-volume, low-return marketing efforts**.

1. **Increased Campaign Efficiency**

   > *Example:* A dermatology practice **streamlined its branding**, creating **consistent social media templates and ad formats**. This **cut ad design time in half,** reducing their **marketing spend by 20%.**

2. **Improved Audience Engagement**

   > *Example:* A pediatric clinic **redesigned its website and branding** to emphasize a **warm, child-friendly environment**. Engagement on social media **jumped by 40%**, leading to **more patient referrals without additional ad spend**.

3. **Strengthened Word-of-Mouth Referrals**
   Patients who **connect with a brand are more likely to refer it.** A **well-branded practice** naturally **attracts organic referrals**, reducing **reliance on paid ads.**

> *Example:* A wellness chain that **unified its branding** across **social media, in-office signage, and patient communication** reduced ad spend by **20% while increasing new patient acquisition by 35%.**

Actionable Steps to Optimize Marketing Spend

- ☐ Develop a Comprehensive Brand Guide:
  Ensure all materials **follow consistent logo specifications, color palettes, typography, and messaging frameworks.**
- ☐ Streamline Marketing Materials:
  Use **templates and pre-approved assets** to maintain cohesion across all campaigns.
- ☐ Invest in Quality Over Quantity:
  Focus on **fewer, high-impact campaigns** rather than spreading resources across **multiple uncoordinated efforts.**
- ☐ Leverage Digital Marketing Tools:
  Use **Google Analytics and Facebook Ads Manager** to track **campaign performance**, refine strategy, and reduce waste.
- ☐ Test and Optimize Campaigns Regularly:
  Use **A/B testing** to identify the **most effective messaging and visuals** to **maximize ROI.**

The Cost of Inaction

Practices that **fail to invest in branding** often find themselves caught in a **cycle of wasteful spending. Poor branding leads to diminished returns** on marketing investments, forcing businesses to **allocate more resources just to maintain visibility.**

Over time, this **hinders growth, profitability, and long-term sustainability.**

A well-defined **brand strategy** is a cost-saving tool, helping practices **reduce marketing expenses, increase patient engagement, and drive long-term profitability**.

Conclusion: Branding as a Cost-Saving Measure

Branding isn't just about **looks**—it's a **financial strategy**. A **clear, consistent brand** improves **marketing efficiency, strengthens patient engagement, and drives better ROI**. By **investing in a cohesive brand strategy,** health and wellness practices can **cut marketing costs, achieve better results, and build a more profitable future**.

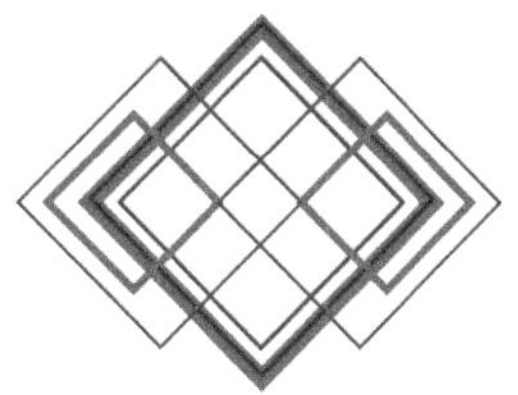

CHAPTER 5

Reputational Damage

In the health and wellness industry, reputation is everything. Patients entrust their health and well-being to providers, expecting professionalism, consistency, and care at every interaction. Branding is not just about marketing—it is the **foundation of a practice's reputation**. A strong brand reinforces trust, while poor branding creates confusion, mistrust, and dissatisfaction. When branding is inconsistent, misleading, or does not align with the patient experience, the consequences can be severe, leading to lost patients, negative reviews, and a tarnished reputation that is difficult to repair.

A study by PwC revealed that **50% of patients would stop using a healthcare provider after just one negative experience** *(PwC, 2023)*. This underscores the fragile nature of trust in healthcare. In an era where a single online review can go viral in hours, reputational damage can spread rapidly, making it critical for practices to ensure that their branding and patient experience align.

The Branding Ripple Effect: How One Patient's Experience Shapes Public Perception

Imagine a patient named Sarah searching for a new dermatologist. She finds a practice with a sleek, modern website that highlights cutting-edge treatments and personalized care. Impressed, she books an appointment. However, when she arrives, the office is outdated, the staff appears disengaged, and the provider rushes through her consultation without answering her questions. Disappointed, Sarah leaves a one-star review detailing her experience.

Within days, her review gained traction, with other patients chiming in to share similar frustrations. The practice's **Google rating drops below 4.0**, reducing new **patient inquiries by nearly 30%** *(PatientPop, 2023)*. The impact doesn't stop there—Sarah tells her friends, coworkers, and family about her poor experience, reinforcing the perception that this clinic overpromises but underdelivers.

This scenario illustrates how branding isn't just about logos and marketing materials—it's about the **entire patient experience**. A strong brand aligns what a practice says with what it actually delivers. When there's a disconnect, it doesn't just impact one patient—it triggers a ripple effect that can reshape public perception and diminish long-term trust.

Expert Insights: What Industry Leaders Say About Branding and Reputation

Branding experts in the healthcare space emphasize the importance of consistency and trust in shaping reputation:

> *"Your brand is more than your logo or your tagline—it's the sum of every experience a patient has with your practice. When branding and reality don't align, patients feel deceived, and trust is nearly impossible to rebuild."*
> **— Dr. Michael Levin, Healthcare Marketing Strategist**

> *"A well-managed brand can reduce marketing costs by*

> *up to 20% because strong word-of-mouth and reputation act as natural patient acquisition tools."*
> **— Sarah Kim, Brand Consultant for Health & Wellness Providers**

> *"Patients don't buy services; they buy trust. If your branding sets an expectation that your patient experience doesn't meet, you're actively driving patients away."*
> **— James Redding, Founder of Patient-First Branding Agency**

When Branding Fails: Case Studies in Reputational Damage

The Social Media Illusion: How a Strong Online Presence Masked a Poor In-Person Experience

A weight-loss clinic in California had a polished social media presence filled with inspiring success stories and professional-looking facilities. However, patients arriving at the clinic found outdated equipment, rushed staff, and an impersonal experience. The disconnect between the **expectations set by branding** and the **actual patient experience** led to a surge of negative reviews, dropping the clinic's Google rating from 4.2 to 3.1 within six months and reducing inquiries by 22%.

This case highlights a critical branding lesson: **perception must match reality**. Patients expect honesty, and when branding overpromises, trust erodes quickly.

A Luxury Wellness Retreat That Was Anything But Luxurious

A Colorado-based wellness retreat promoted itself as an elite, five-star escape from stress, featuring high-end spa treatments and personalized care. However, guests arrived to find outdated accommodations, understaffed facilities, and misleading pricing. Customers took to social media, posting side-by-side comparisons of the glossy marketing materials versus the reality they encountered.

The backlash resulted in over $100,000 in cancellations and

refunds, a tarnished online reputation, and a costly rebranding effort. The key takeaway? **Exaggerating brand promises may attract customers initially, but it will drive them away just as quickly when expectations aren't met.**

The Chiropractic Clinic That Lost Trust Due to Outdated Branding

A chiropractic clinic positioned itself as a leader in advanced spinal care, promoting cutting-edge techniques. However, upon arrival, patients found an outdated facility with aging equipment and minimal technology integration. This **misalignment between brand messaging and real-world experience** led to a 30% drop in retention rates and a 15% decline in referrals within a year. Ultimately, the clinic had to invest significantly in updating its infrastructure and revising its branding to rebuild credibility.

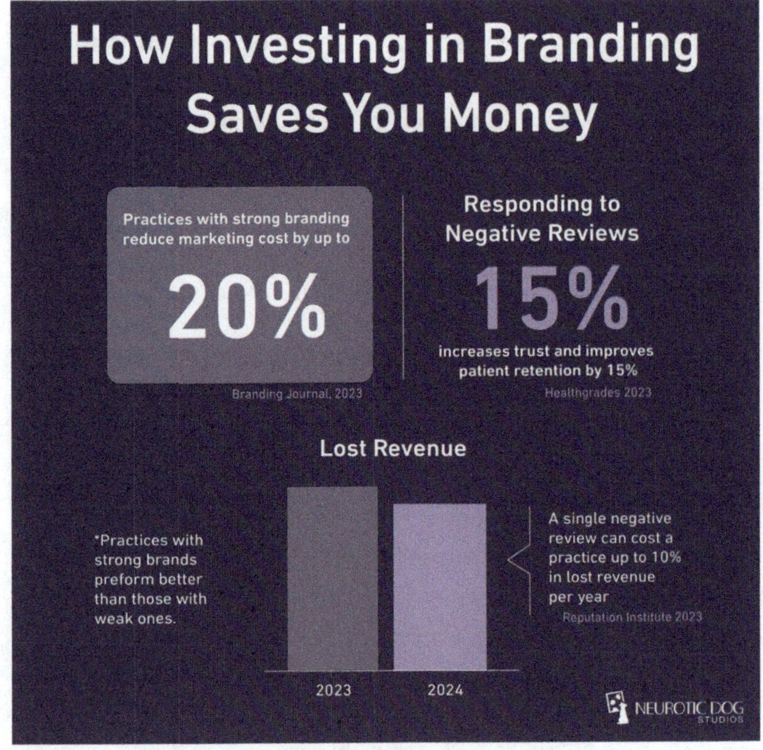

Strategies for Proactively Managing Reputation Through Branding

A strong brand can mitigate reputational damage and build long-term trust. To ensure alignment:

- ☐ **Conduct Regular Brand Audits:** Evaluate whether marketing materials, patient experiences, and online presence reflect your core values.
- ☐ **Train Staff to Embody Your Brand's Values:** Ensure that employees—from front-desk personnel to medical professionals—deliver a patient experience that aligns with branding promises.
- ☐ **Manage Online Reviews Proactively:** Respond to both positive and negative feedback, demonstrating a commitment to continuous improvement.
- ☐ **Align Physical and Digital Branding:** Your website, social media, office environment, and patient communications should tell a cohesive story.

Research shows that businesses with strong branding recover from reputation crises 50% faster than those with weak branding *(Forbes, 2023)*. Moreover, 75% of consumers judge a business's credibility based on its website design alone *(Adobe, 2023)*, proving that first impressions matter long before a patient ever steps into your office.

Self-Check: Is Your Branding Protecting Your Reputation?

1. Does your practice's branding align with the actual patient experience?
2. Are staff trained to reinforce your brand's message through patient interactions?
3. Are you consistently managing your online reputation, responding to reviews, and making improvements?
4. Have you implemented patient satisfaction initiatives to ensure ongoing trust and loyalty?

If the answer to any of these is "no," now is the time to take action. Branding isn't just about marketing—it's about trust, credibility, and long-term success.

Conclusion: Branding as a Safeguard for Reputation

Your reputation is your most valuable asset. A well-defined brand does more than attract patients—it fosters loyalty, trust, and sustainable growth. Branding misalignment can lead to reputational damage that is difficult and costly to repair. By ensuring that branding accurately reflects patient experiences, healthcare providers can protect their credibility, maintain patient trust, and build a lasting legacy of excellence.

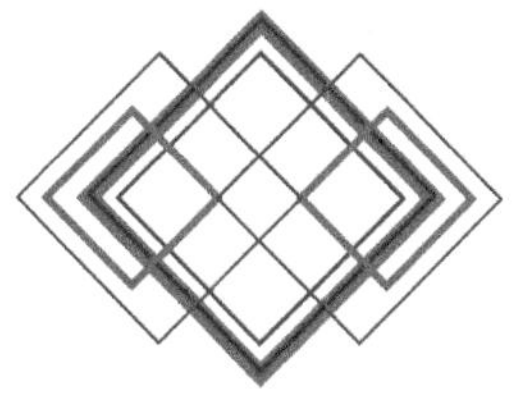

CHAPTER 6

The Long-Term Implications

Branding is not just a short-term strategy—it's an investment in the future of your health and wellness practice. While the immediate impacts of poor branding, such as reduced patient inquiries or negative reviews, may seem manageable at first, the long-term consequences can erode the foundation of your practice. From missed growth opportunities to declining patient retention and operational inefficiencies, weak branding can create a downward spiral that's difficult to reverse.

Why Branding Is a Long-Term Asset

A strong brand provides stability, adaptability, and scalability. It becomes the framework through which patients, employees, and partners interact with your practice, creating trust and consistency that endures. Without a cohesive brand, practices struggle to maintain relevance, attract new patients, or evolve alongside industry changes. According to McKinsey, companies with strong branding are **20% more likely to outperform their competitors** in market share growth over ten years. This highlights the critical role branding plays in long-term sustainability.

The Long-Term Costs of Poor Branding

Stagnant Growth

Poor branding limits a practice's ability to expand into new markets or introduce additional services. Patients may perceive the practice as outdated or incapable of handling growth.

For example, a wellness center that lacked consistency in its brand messaging struggled to attract investors for expansion. The inconsistency in marketing materials, logo variations, and conflicting messaging made it difficult for investors to see a clear, professional vision for the practice's future. Without a defined and reliable brand, financial backers hesitated, resulting in missed funding opportunities that stalled growth.

Declining Patient Retention

Brand loyalty is built over time. Patients who feel no emotional connection to a practice are more likely to explore other options. Weak branding fails to communicate values and mission effectively, leading to a decline in long-term patient relationships. Research by PwC found that **practices with strong patient retention, driven by branding, see a 50% higher lifetime value per patient** *(PwC, 2023).*

Increased Competition

In competitive markets, the practices with the strongest brands consistently capture more patients. Without a well-defined brand, a practice risks becoming just another option instead of a preferred provider.

A dental office in a suburban area lost market share to a newer competitor that presented a **cohesive, modern brand** emphasizing **patient comfort, cutting-edge technology, and seamless digital experiences.** The established practice, while experienced, had an outdated brand identity that failed to engage younger, tech-savvy patients. Within three years, the new competitor had overtaken the older practice in online search rankings and patient volume.

Reduced Adaptability

A strong brand is the foundation that allows a practice to pivot and evolve with industry changes. Practices without a clear brand identity struggle to adapt to shifting patient expectations, emerging technology, and new market trends. Without a recognizable and adaptable brand, any effort to modernize services or enter new spaces feels disconnected and inconsistent.

Operational Inefficiencies

Poor branding doesn't just affect marketing—it impacts **every internal process.** Without a strong brand framework, efforts are often duplicated, misaligned, or wasted. Onboarding new staff, launching promotional campaigns, and updating internal systems become chaotic when branding lacks clarity. **Brand infrastructure—such as defined messaging, style guides, and digital assets—creates a foundation for efficiency.**

Real-Life Examples of Long-Term Branding Challenges

Case Study: Missed Growth Opportunities

A holistic therapy center aimed to launch **telehealth services during the pandemic** but lacked the branding infrastructure to market and onboard patients effectively. Their website and marketing materials were inconsistent, with outdated fonts, varying color schemes, and unclear messaging about virtual services. While competitors with streamlined branding immediately capitalized on telehealth demand, this practice lost momentum, allowing the market to become saturated before they had positioned themselves properly.

> *Impact:* The practice missed an estimated **$200,000 in po-**

> **tential revenue** over two years due to slow adoption and weak brand positioning.

Case Study: Struggling to Stay Relevant
A mid-sized health clinic with a longstanding reputation in its community failed to modernize its brand over time. The clinic relied on **outdated visuals, inconsistent messaging, and an antiquated online booking system.** Over the years, younger patients gravitated toward competitors that offered **seamless digital experiences, mobile scheduling, and strong social media engagement.**

> *Impact:* Within five years, patient volume declined by **30%**, forcing the clinic to invest heavily in digital transformation just to stay competitive.

Industry Data: Branding's Role in Long-Term Success

- Over **80% of businesses focusing on long-term brand-building** report **sustained growth** and **higher profitability** compared to those that prioritize short-term tactics *(Kantar, 2023).*
- Companies that consistently update and invest in their branding are **25% more resilient during economic downturns** *(Harvard Business Review, 2023).*
- Practices with strong patient retention see a **50% higher lifetime value per patient** *(PwC, 2023).*

How Strong Branding Drives Long-Term Success

Creates Emotional Connections
Over time, patients build trust with brands that remain **consistent and engaging**. Branding that reflects patient values fosters loyalty, encouraging repeat visits and referrals.

Enables Scalability
A well-defined brand makes it easier to expand into new mar-

kets, introduce new services, and **maintain brand consistency across multiple locations**.

Future-Proofs the Practice
Brands that evolve **with industry shifts** and **patient expectations** remain competitive. Modernization is easier when a brand foundation is **solid and adaptable**.

Reduces Marketing and Recruitment Costs
A consistent brand streamlines marketing campaigns and attracts top-tier talent who align with its mission, reducing the need for costly recruitment efforts.

Actionable Steps to Ensure Long-Term Branding Success

- ☐ **Commit to Regular Brand Audits**: Evaluate your brand's effectiveness at least once a year, ensuring its relevance, consistency, and alignment with patient expectations.
- ☐ **Stay Ahead of Industry Trends**: Monitor changes in patient behavior, technology, and market dynamics to maintain a **competitive brand identity**.
- ☐ **Invest in Brand Storytelling**: Build a compelling brand narrative that evolves with your practice. Highlight milestones, patient successes, and your **commitment to innovation**.
- ☐ **Integrate Branding into Strategic Planning:** Ensure that branding isn't just a marketing effort but a core element of long-term business strategy.
- ☐ **Engage Employees in Brand Evolution**: Your staff should be part of branding discussions, ensuring internal alignment and brand advocacy.

The Cost of Neglecting Long-Term Branding

Failing to prioritize branding results in **missed opportunities for growth, declining patient loyalty, and increased vulnerability to competition.** Without a clear brand identity, practices are **less equipped to handle industry disruptions or capitalize on emerging trends**, ultimately putting their **long-term survival at risk.**

Real-World Impact: Branding During Economic Uncertainty

A wellness chain that **invested in a rebrand during an economic downturn** saw a **20% increase in patient retention** and **secured new investors**, allowing it to **expand into three new markets**. Meanwhile, competitors that delayed branding efforts struggled to regain lost ground.

Conclusion: Branding as a Legacy

In the health and wellness industry, branding is more than just a marketing tool—it's the foundation of a **sustainable, resilient practice**. A strong brand ensures that your practice remains **relevant, trusted, and adaptable**, allowing you to grow and thrive for years to come. By **investing in long-term branding**, you're not just securing your current success—you're building a **lasting legacy**.

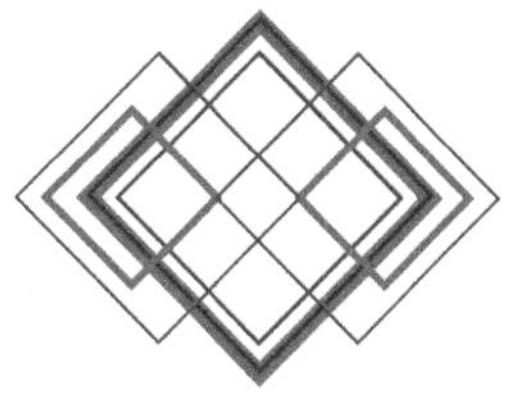

CHAPTER 7

Identifying Branding Gaps

To address the hidden costs of poor branding, health, and wellness practices must first identify where their brand is failing. Gaps can manifest in various ways, such as unprofessional visuals, inconsistent messaging, or an unclear value proposition. Identifying these weaknesses is the first step toward building a strong, cohesive brand that fosters trust, loyalty, and growth.

Why Identifying Gaps Is Critical

Branding is the foundation of how patients perceive your practice. Gaps create confusion, erode trust, and diminish the overall patient experience. By identifying and addressing these gaps, you ensure every aspect of your practice aligns with your mission, values, and goals. client

Key Insight:

According to Lucidpress, **81% of businesses report inconsistent branding damages their reputation and reduces patient trust.** This highlights the importance of scheduled audits of your brand to ensure alignment and consistency.

Common Gaps in Health and Wellness Practices

Visual Identity

When a practice's logo, colors, and typography are inconsistent across different platforms, it creates a fragmented experience that can make a business appear unprofessional. For example, a dental practice that used one set of standards on its website but a different style on brochures left patients questioning the clinic's professionalism. The lack of cohesion suggested disorganization, making potential patients hesitant to trust their services.

Messaging

A clear, consistent message builds trust with patients, but when communication styles and strategies vary across platforms, it can create confusion and reduce credibility. A wellness clinic, for instance, promoted itself online as a leader in holistic care but ran social media campaigns that focused on discounts and promotions. The disconnect between its supposed mission and its marketing made potential patients question the depth of its expertise and commitment to holistic wellness.

Patient Experience

Branding extends beyond visuals and messaging—it's also about the experience patients receive. A spa that advertised itself as a high-end luxury retreat but failed to maintain its facilities and ambiance created a jarring disconnect. Patients who expected a serene, upscale environment were met with outdated décor and inattentive service, leading to poor reviews and a decline in repeat visits.

Engagement

Engagement is crucial for patient loyalty, yet many practices fail to maintain consistent communication. A physical therapy clinic with a strong brand presence on its website but neglected online reviews and rarely engaged with patient inquiries lost credibility. Patients who left comments or complaints online were met with silence, making them feel undervalued and pushing them toward competitors who actively engaged with their audience.

Internal Alignment
Employees are an essential part of a brand, and when they don't understand or embody the brand's values, it creates a disconnect that affects patient experience. A medical clinic that prided itself on being "patient-centered" but had a front desk staff known for being dismissive and rushed created a clear misalignment. The contradiction between branding promises and patient interactions led to frustrated patients and declining retention rates.

Real-Life Examples

Case Study: A Chiropractic Office's Disjointed Marketing
A chiropractic office realized its social media posts, patient forms, and in-office decor used different color schemes and fonts. After conducting a brand audit, they unified their visual identity, creating a more professional and cohesive patient experience.

> *Outcome:* Patient satisfaction scores improved by **20%**, and referrals increased by **15%** within six months.

Case Study: Messaging Misalignment at a Weight-Loss Clinic
A weight-loss clinic advertised itself as offering "comprehensive wellness," but its services focused solely on diet plans. The disconnect frustrated patients and resulted in negative reviews. The clinic restored trust and clarity by refining its messaging to focus on its core offering.

> *Outcome:* The clinic's Google rating improved from **3.5 to 4.2 stars**, leading to a **25% increase** in new patient inquiries.

How to Conduct a Brand Audit

A brand audit involves evaluating your practices visuals (logo, website, marketing assets), messaging (any written word, audio spots or vidso), and patient interactions. Use the following checklist to assess your brand's effectiveness:

- ☐ Is your logo modern, professional, and aligned with your values?
- ☐ Do your website, brochures, and social media use consistent colors, fonts, and imagery?
- ☐ Does your messaging communicate your unique value proposition clearly and consistently?
- ☐ Does your patient experience align with your purpose, mission, vision, values and the promises they present (either expressed or implied) to your patients?
- ☐ Are employees trained to represent your brand in every interaction?

Gathering Feedback from Patients and Staff

Soliciting input from patients and staff provides valuable insight into how your brand is perceived. Use surveys, interviews, or suggestion boxes to identify gaps and areas for improvement.

Reviewing Competitors

Compare your branding to that of competitors in your area. Identify what they're doing well, and what they are not. You may find areas where you are lacking, but you may also discover gaps you can fill. Learning from industry leaders can highlight opportunities to refine and strengthen your brand. Word of caution: **Do NOT copy them.** You are not them, and they are not you.You may learn something from them you can implement - but is must be in alignment and authentic to you, not because it's successful for them.

Evaluating Patient Experience

Walk through the **patient journey,** from booking an appointment to follow-ups. Identify gaps where the experience doesn't align with your brand promise and adjust accordingly.

Analyzing Online Presence

Review your **website, social media, and online reviews**. Inconsistent posting, negative feedback, or outdated content may indicate a gaps. Regular updates and engagement can rebuild trust and improve brand perception.

Industry Data

- **77% of patients** say an unprofessional website damages their perception of a practice. *(Adobe, 2023)*
- Companies with **inconsistent branding experience 25% lower revenue growth** than those with cohesive branding. *(Forrester, 2023)*
- **Practices that have scheduled audits of their branding** report **30% higher patient retention rates.** *(Nielsen, 2023)*

Tools

- ☐ **Google Analytics:** Use analytics to assess your website's performance. High bounce rates may indicate poor design or irrelevant content.
- ☐ **Social Media Insights:** Review engagement metrics to identify which posts resonate with your audience and where improvements are needed.
- ☐ **Brand Consistency Tools:** Platforms like **Lucidpress** or **Canva Pro** help standardize visuals across platforms, reducing inconsistencies.
- ☐ **Patient Feedback Surveys:** Tools like **SurveyMonkey** or **Typeform** allow you to gather actionable patient feedback about their experiences and perceptions.

Actionable Steps

- **Create a Unified Brand Guide**
  Develop a comprehensive guide that includes **your logo, color palette, fonts, tone of voice, and messaging framework.** Please share it with all staff and partners to ensure consistency.

- **Align Internal Culture**
  Train staff on your **brand values** and how to reflect them in patient interactions. Regular team meetings can reinforce these principles.

- **Refine Messaging Across Platforms**
  Ensure your **website, social media, and print materials** communicate the same value proposition and tone, eliminating mixed messaging.

- **Invest in Professional Design**
  Work with branding experts to modernize **outdated logos, websites, or marketing materials** that may diminish your credibility.

- **Track Progress**
  Set measurable goals for improving patient perception, such as increasing **Google ratings or boosting referral rates.** Regularly monitor progress and adjust as needed.

Conclusion: The Foundation for Success

Identifying any gaps you may have is the first step toward building a **strong, cohesive brand** that resonates with patients and drives **long-term growth**. By taking a proactive approach, health and wellness practices can **close these gaps, enhance patient experiences, and create a brand that stands** out in a competitive market..

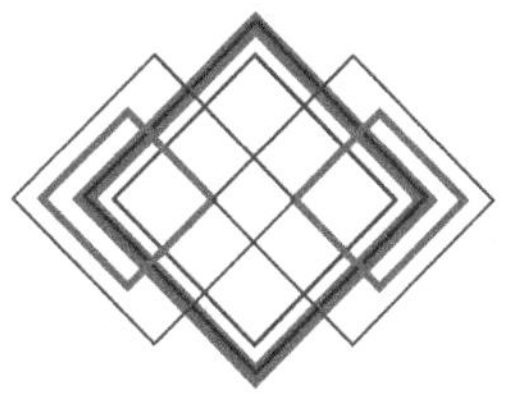

CHAPTER 8

Strategies to Overcome Poor Branding

Poor branding can feel overwhelming, especially for health and wellness practices already balancing patient care and daily operations. However, a well-structured approach can transform branding weaknesses into strengths. By implementing clear strategies, practices can rebuild trust, attract new patients, and foster long-term growth.

Define Your Unique Value Proposition (UVP)

Your UVP is the foundation of your brand, setting you apart from competitors and communicating the unique benefits you offer. Without a well-defined UVP, branding becomes vague and forgettable and fails to attract the right patients. Identifying your target audience, understanding their needs, and articulating what makes your practice unique will shape a compelling UVP.

A chiropractic clinic, for example, struggled to differentiate itself from local competitors. By refining its UVP from the generic "We help people feel better" to "A family-focused chiropractic clinic specializing in pain relief and mobility solutions tailored to active lifestyles," the practice saw a 20% increase in new patient inquiries within six months.

Invest in Professional Design

A strong visual identity is crucial in making a positive first impression. Outdated logos, inconsistent color schemes, and disjointed typography can make your practice appear unprofessional or untrustworthy. Investing in professional design ensures consistency across all branding materials, from your website and social media to patient forms and office signage.

A wellness clinic, for instance, modernized its logo to emphasize holistic care, adopted a calming color palette of greens and blues, and redesigned its website for a seamless user experience. The result? A 30% increase in patient inquiries within three months.

Before - Medical Access rebranded to trüHealthNow - After

Align Branding with Patient Experience

Your brand is more than just visuals—it's the full experience patients have when interacting with your practice. Trust erodes when branding promises do not align with reality, leading to dissatisfaction and patient churn. Training staff to embody brand values and to ensure every touchpoint aligns with your messaging is critical.

Companies with cohesive branding across all platforms see an average 33% increase in marketing ROI. *(Source: Lucidpress)*

Engage in Authentic Storytelling

Patients connect with stories, not statistics. Sharing your journey, values, and patient success stories makes your brand relatable and fosters deeper emotional connections. Authentic storytelling should be woven into marketing materials, social media content, and your website to create a compelling brand narrative.

Organizations that actively engage in brand storytelling report 22x more reach and engagement than those relying on traditional marketing. *(Source: Nielsen)*

Monitor and Adapt Your Brand

Branding is not a one-time effort—it evolves alongside patient expectations and industry trends. Regular brand audits help identify areas for improvement, ensuring your messaging remains relevant and effective.

70% of patients say they're more likely to choose a healthcare provider with a modern, professional brand. *(Source: PatientPop).*

Leverage Technology for Branding Efficiency

Technology streamlines branding efforts, making maintaining consistency and measuring impact easier. Tools like **Canva** or **Adobe Spark** allow practices to create branded visuals quickly, while automation platforms such as **Hootsuite** or **Buffer** help schedule and maintain a steady social media presence.

A chiropractic clinic struggling with social media engagement implemented an automated scheduling system for consistent, branded content. Within a few months, the clinic saw a **25% increase** in follower growth and higher patient inquiries, proving the value of streamlined branding efforts.

Actionable Framework for Overcoming Poor Branding

1. **Audit Your Branding**
   Use a checklist to evaluate your visuals, messaging, and patient experience for consistency and alignment.

2. **Create a Brand Guide**
   Standardize your branding efforts by including logo specifications, tone of voice, color palettes, and messaging frameworks.

3. **Train Staff on Branding**
   Hold workshops or training sessions to ensure your team understands and embodies brand values in every patient interaction.

4. **Invest in Quality Marketing**
   Work with professionals to create high-quality, branded materials that resonate with your target audience.

5. **Measure Progress**
   Set measurable goals, such as increasing Google ratings or patient referrals, and track progress over time.

Conclusion: Transforming Weakness into Opportunity

Poor branding isn't the end—it's an opportunity to rebuild and refine. By implementing these strategies, health and wellness practices can overcome branding challenges, strengthen their reputations, and create lasting connections with patients. Investing in your brand today ensures a more profitable, resilient practice tomorrow.

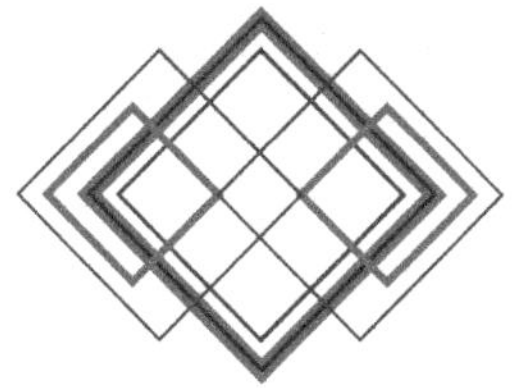

CHAPTER 9

Building a Sustainable Brand

In the health and wellness industry, your brand is more than a logo or a marketing tool—it's your practice's identity and reputation. It communicates who you are, what you stand for, and why patients should trust you. While the hidden costs of poor branding can feel overwhelming, they also present an opportunity to rebuild, refine, and strengthen your practice. A well-crafted, sustainable brand does more than attract patients—it fosters trust, cultivates loyalty, and drives long-term growth.

The Importance of Proactive Branding

Branding isn't a one-time effort. It requires ongoing attention, adaptation, and investment to remain relevant in an ever-changing healthcare landscape. Practices that prioritize their brand build stronger relationships with patients, differentiate themselves from competitors, and create a foundation for sustained success.

Key Insight:

A *Harvard Business Review* study found that **64% of consum-**

ers build relationships with brands based on shared values and consistent messaging. For health and wellness practices, every patient interaction, marketing campaign, and service offering must align with the brand's mission and vision.

The Benefits of Investing in Your Brand

Increased Patient Loyalty

A strong, consistent brand fosters **emotional connections** with patients, making them **more likely to return and refer others.** Patients trust brands that feel familiar, reliable, and aligned with their personal values.

Stronger Competitive Positioning

With healthcare choices expanding, a well-defined brand ensures your practice **stands out.** Competing on price alone isn't sustainable—**competing on trust, expertise, and experience is.**

Improved Employee Engagement

Branding isn't just external—it's internal, too. Employees who understand and **embrace a practice's mission and values are more motivated, engaged, and committed to delivering exceptional care**.

Scalability and Adaptability

A strong brand provides the **flexibility to grow**, whether expanding into new markets, introducing additional services, or adapting to shifting patient expectations.

Key Takeaways

- **Poor branding erodes trust and loyalty**, leading to fewer patient inquiries, lower retention rates, and reduced referrals.
- **Inconsistent branding increases marketing expenses**, requiring more resources to achieve minimal results.

- **Weak branding damages your reputation**, making attracting and retaining patients long-term harder.
- **Investing in professional branding creates a cohesive identity**, improving patient engagement, loyalty, and revenue.
- **Regular brand audits ensure continued relevance and competitiveness**, helping practices adapt to industry changes.

Next Steps: Implementing a Sustainable Brand Strategy

To build a brand that resonates with patients and supports long-term growth, follow these actionable steps:

1. **Conduct a Comprehensive Brand Audit**
   Evaluate your visual identity, messaging, patient experience, and online presence to identify inconsistencies and areas for improvement. Use patient surveys, staff feedback, and online analytics to gather insights.

2. **Create a Unified Brand Guide**
   Develop a branding playbook that standardizes your **logo, color palette, typography, tone of voice, and messaging framework.** This ensures consistency across all platforms—website, social media, marketing materials, and in-office signage.

3. **Engage Your Team in Branding Efforts**
   Train staff on the practice's mission and values, empowering them to embody the brand in every patient interaction. When employees feel aligned with the brand, they become powerful ambassadors, reinforcing its credibility.

4. **Leverage Technology for Brand Management**
   Utilize digital tools to maintain branding consistency, monitor online reputation, and track marketing effective-

ness. Platforms like **Google Analytics, Hootsuite, Canva, and Reputation.com** help streamline branding efforts and ensure engagement with your audience.

5. **Commit to Ongoing Brand Evaluation**
   Revisit and refine your brand strategy regularly. Stay aware of patient expectations, industry trends, and competitor positioning to ensure your brand remains strong and relevant.

Real-World Impact: A Case Study in Brand Transformation

A mid-sized dermatology clinic struggled with inconsistent branding, leading to lower patient retention and weak online engagement. After conducting a brand audit, they implemented a cohesive rebranding strategy—updating their logo, refining messaging to emphasize patient-centered care, and training staff to reflect the brand's core values. Within **one year**, the clinic saw a **35% increase in patient referrals,** a **20% improvement in staff satisfaction scores,** and a **higher online review rating** from **3.9 to 4.6 stars**.

Transform Your Brand Today

At **Neurotic Dog Studios**, we help health and wellness practices overcome branding challenges and create strong, sustainable identities that inspire trust, loyalty, and growth. Whether you're refining an existing brand or building from the ground up, we provide the expertise and tools to help you succeed.

Contact us today to schedule a consultation and take the first step toward developing a brand that genuinely represents your practice's mission and values.

Final Thought: Branding as a Legacy

Your brand is more than just your logo or website—it's the

story, promise, and experience you create for your patients. A sustainable brand ensures your practice remains relevant, resilient, and thriving in an evolving healthcare landscape. The costs of weak branding are significant, but the **rewards of getting it right**—higher patient trust, more substantial growth, and long-term stability—are immeasurable.

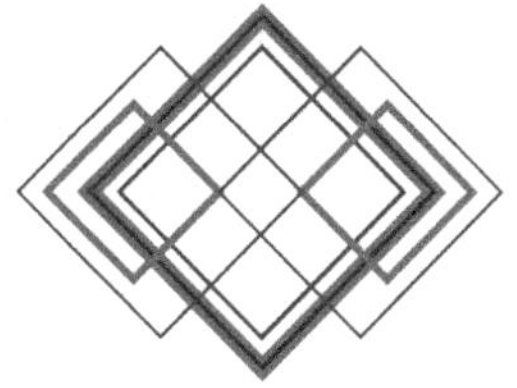

CHAPTER 10

Your Path to a Powerful Brand

Branding isn't just about design or catchy slogans—it's about creating a legacy of trust, loyalty, and growth. As a health and wellness provider, you're not simply running a business; you're building relationships, changing lives, and leaving an indelible mark on your community. Every choice you make about your brand shapes how patients perceive and connect with you. A strong, cohesive brand amplifies that impact, helping you attract the right patients and sustain your practice in an ever-evolving industry.

Why Now Is the Time to Act

Branding is not a passive element of your practice—it's an active force that either propels you forward or holds you back. Each day without a clear, consistent brand is a missed opportunity. It's a patient choosing another provider because your website felt outdated. It's a referral lost because your messaging didn't communicate confidence and expertise. It's an employee who feels disengaged because the mission isn't clear.

The good news? You have the power to change that narrative. The right brand strategy transforms branding from an overlooked detail into a powerful driver of trust, connection, and growth.

Key Insight:
A **Forrester** study found that **health and wellness practices that invest in branding see a 33% increase in patient retention and 20% higher revenues over three years.** Your brand is more than a logo—it's a key player in your success story.

The Opportunity Ahead

Whether you're modernizing your brand or starting from scratch, this is your moment to take control of your identity. A well-crafted brand isn't just a visual asset—it's a strategic foundation that defines how your patients, staff, and community perceive you. A strong brand allows you to:

- **Attract patients who align with your values.** People seek healthcare providers they trust. A clear brand message helps patients know if you're the right fit for them.
- **Build trust that fosters long-term loyalty.** Patients stay with providers who deliver not only quality care but also a reassuring, consistent experience.
- **Create a competitive advantage in your market.** In a crowded industry, branding is often the deciding factor when patients are choosing between providers.
- **Communicate your expertise, professionalism, and care.** Your brand tells patients why they should choose you over the competition.

Your Next Steps: Turning Vision into Action

1. **Reflect on Your Brand Vision**
   Before making changes, define your purpose. What do

you want patients to feel, think, and remember about your practice? Your vision should be the foundation of all branding decisions.

> *Imagine this:* A pediatric wellness center wants to be known as a comforting, fun environment for children and their families. Their branding should reflect that—not just in colors and logos but in every aspect of the patient experience, from waiting room decor to appointment reminders.

2. **Audit Your Branding**
   Conduct a **brand audit** to evaluate how well your current brand aligns with your vision. Look at your **website, social media, office signage, patient materials, and even employee messaging.** Are they consistent? Do they tell a cohesive story?

   A holistic therapy clinic discovered that while their mission focused on personalized, patient-centered care, their outdated website and impersonal marketing materials didn't reflect that. After refining their messaging and updating their design, they saw a 40% increase in new patient inquiries.

3. **Partner with Branding Experts**
   Branding is both an art and a science. It requires **insight, strategy, and creativity**—and most healthcare professionals don't have the time to master it on their own. Collaborate with professionals who understand your industry, market positioning, and patient psychology to create a brand that speaks directly to your ideal audience.

4. **Implement and Evolve**
   Branding isn't a one-time event; it's an ongoing process. Once your brand is refined, integrate it across every touch-

point:

- Train your team to embody the brand's values in every patient interaction.
- Ensure your website, signage, and printed materials consistently reflect your identity.
- Engage with patients through social media and educational content that aligns with your brand voice.
- Monitor patient feedback and online reputation to ensure your brand is resonating as intended.

A Word of Encouragement

Building a powerful brand is a journey, not a destination. It requires commitment, adaptation, and continuous effort—but the rewards are undeniable. Your practice has a unique story, a dedicated team, and a mission that deserves to be seen and celebrated. By investing in your brand, you're investing in the future of your patients, employees, and community.

You don't have to navigate this journey alone. Branding is a strategic asset—one that, when cultivated correctly, becomes a driving force behind your success. The time to take action is now.

Final Thought: The Path to a Powerful Brand Starts Today

A sustainable brand is more than just a logo or tagline—it's the **experience, promise, and legacy** you create. In a world where trust is everything, a strong brand ensures your practice remains **top-of-mind, top-of-choice, and built for long-term success.**

Are you ready to take control of your brand? Your next chapter begins today.

CHAPTER 11

Alice Pettey, Author

I don't know about you, but I have always hated writing the "about" section.

I mean, really, what do you want to know or even care about? Should I list my credentials and accolades? They can sound great, right? But, then again, that could sound pompous and egotistical & hey, do you care that I graduated Valedictorian of my Master's program or that I'm a certified brand strategist? Maybe you want to know how I got here and the why behind it all. It's not an exciting story. It has a bit of tragedy and frustration woven through, but if you're up for it & want to know, here goes.

Where Does the Story Start?

I guess after college makes sense. Of course, by then, I'd already set aside my dreams for the realities of having two children to support. There is nothing revolutionary here, just youthful spur-of-the-moment decisions that result in lifelong consequences – you know, life. It led me to my first full-time position with an interior design agency.

I worked as the receptionist/office manager for the firm but was exposed to a new world of experience, not in designing office layouts but in using the technology. I found this fascinating. So, just two years after receiving my Bachelor of Arts (in History, no less), I enrolled in Graphic Design and Multimedia courses. This was way back in 1999, but I found programs could be taken entirely online.

Once I got a foundation for the software and the basic concepts of design, I dug in deep—through every book, training program, video, seminar, well, anything I could think of or get my hands on to expand my understanding of design and creativity. I learned that there was design, and then there was DESIGN. Anyone can do design.

Today, that's what Canva is for – making design accessible & it's great. It provides templates and frameworks to non-designers to create pieces that look good & fulfill their needs without having to devote the hours and expense of hiring or learning design. Then there is DESIGN. This is not about making things look nice but about approaching things from a strategic and business focus. It's about communication and fulfilling business goals.

I was [and still am] excited about this form of design —"strategic design," and how it must be brought into the process SO much earlier and not viewed as the afterthought to "make things pretty." But 9-11 happens, businesses downsize, and as I expecting my third child, I'm an easy layoff. It was a fun Christmas that year. Come April, we welcomed our youngest son into the family, and life was never the same..

A Shift In Focus And Change In Priorities

Our youngest son came with some surprises. We discovered

over his first three years that our baby had Smith-Magenis Syndrome. Our simple explanation is "Autism on steroids," but there is so much more to it; if you're interested, check out PRISMS.org.

With this diagnosis, the direction of our entire family's life changed. The husband and I spent a week in mourning. No one tells you that. You mourn when you get that kind of life-altering diagnosis. You mourn the life you thought you and/or your child were going to have. The plans you made, the dream you didn't even realize you had. Our son wasn't quite three when he was diagnosed, but it's incredible how much of his future I had already dreamed of.

Our daughter, four at our youngest's birth, responded by becoming a little mommy. And she was, right up until the day he died while she & her father tried to save him.

Our oldest son withdrew into himself and suffered severe depression – that we missed because of the constant focus on our youngest. Thankfully, he's still with us.

During the 18-years we had with our youngest, we were blessed with his love, isolated by his condition, ostracized by lack of understanding of his behavior, restricted by obligation and devotion, resentful of limitation, guilt-ridden for our frustration and resentment, overwhelmed by it all, and desperately trying to present a "typical" exterior to the world.

I explored so many healing modalities. I would have gone into that field in another life, but the time and energy required to master any of them truly takes a lifetime, and I recognize my limitations. That is why I greatly respect those who devote themselves to helping others. Western medicine definitely has its place, but I wonder, if we could have invested more into it, would Eastern medicine have made our son's life better? Would it have provided a way to loosened the locked door that he was trapped behind?

I am so angry at one of our local hospitals. We were there a week before our son passed for pre-op (he'd had a dental abscess for 4+ months that they were finally going to address, and given his condition, required an OR); during this check-up, his extremity pulse-ox was 52. I'd never seen them take one on the forehead before – but they managed to get a peak at 93, though typically even that stayed in the 80s & they cleared him for surgery.

Of course, it didn't matter. A week later, we showed up for surgery, and he didn't want to go in. The hospital REFUSED to assist us in getting him into the facility. My husband fought with him for 45 minutes, and I begged for help inside. Finally, we left, and he was dead by mid-afternoon the next day. Nearly four years have passed – I am angry still, not as fiercely as I was, but it's still there.

But anger will not bring my son back. So here I am; nearly four years have passed since his death, and I'm still trying to make sense of it. However, I have decided that I can use my skills to make the world a better place in his memory.

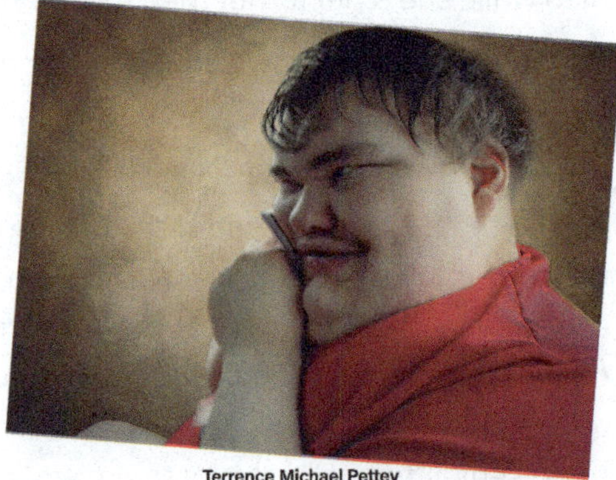

Terrence Michael Pettey

April 29, 2002 – April 7, 2021

Terry Pettey was born at Johnston Willis hospital on April 29, 2002, at 1:51pm. He made his appearance into the world roughly 45 minutes before his cousin. It was a busy day for our family.

Terry was a happy baby, although we did notice a few oddities in his early years. He'd say mama or dada & then lose the word, and he didn't show a startle response to loud noises. We discovered at 12 months that he had massive ear infections and probably had for months, so Terry had tubes put in. Eventually, three sets of them and his adenoids and tonsils removed to help reduce the infections and clear his airway.

By two, Terry was in early intervention at Alberta Smith Elementary. He had two excellent teachers Miss Bess and Miss Amy. If only we could have cloned Miss Bess, our lives would have been so much easier. He loved her & would actually do what he was told with the caveat of "Do we need to tell Miss Bess?" He showed us all his mischievous nature as he would cross his eyes at one of his fellow students just because he knew it would upset him, and he thought it was funny.

At three, Terry was diagnosed with Smith-Magenis Syndrome. This created a massive change in our life as Terry was no longer delayed in his development but permanently disabled. Terry spent his third birthday with his dad and mom in Cincinnati at the PRISMS annual conference. While there, Terry got to meet other SMSers and Drs. Smith & Magenis, the discoverers of Smith-Magenis Syndrome, and participate in 3D facial scanning.

Terry started elementary school at Woolridge Elementary in the Moderate Mentally Disabled class. He continued at Woolridge until his 5th-grade year when it became clear that the public-school environment was not adequate to support his needs.

He transitioned to Grafton, then a short stint at The Faison Center – where they were also not equipped to handle Terry's uniqueness. So back to Grafton, he went where he was loved, cared for, and challenged to grow. Terry has had the support of wonderful teachers and therapists from the Grafton school and was so happy to finally return to in-person learning on March 15 after having spent a year at home due to the pandemic.

Terry spent his last days enjoying spring break by listening to his favorite songs on Spotify, watching YouTube videos, and trying to finagle as many baths with his toy-filled bath bombs as he could.

Terry's Favorites...

Colors: Fluorescent Orange, Red & Blue

Toys: Sully from Monsters Inc. and Buzz Lightyear, anything that came out of his bath bomb, notebooks, ring clips & binder clips

Videos: dominos, roller-coasters, industrial shredders, Spongebob, Power Rangers (in Japanese), Chinese miniature food

Movies: Monster's Inc (#1), Deadpool, The Lion King, Aladdin, Spirit, Mary Poppins Returns, Newsies (or Cowboy's as he called it), Thor Ragnarök (because of the Hulk), the original How the Grinch Stole Christmas

Songs: Shiny (from Moana), Dixie, Big Bad John, The Bad Touch, Airplane, Dirty Harry, North to Alaska, Do Your Ears Hang Low?

Focus And Strategy for The Future

I know branding. Think about your best friend, your spouse, and your significant other. Think about what makes them – them. What they wear. What they listen to. What they sound like. What they smell like. What makes them laugh? What makes them cry? When you walk through a store, some things instantly make you think of them. You have that recognition – that's branding.

It's the conversation, the chance to find clarity, to understand whom you are trying to reach, the concepts – the strategy – behind who you are and why you do what you do. It's not about making it pretty. It's about reaching the right people. It's about understanding why you get up in the morning and go to your practice. It's about understanding whom you're trying to help and why you're trying to help them. It's about communicating that message to them on a daily basis. Solving their problems and letting them know what those problems are before they even realize they have them.

It is innate for every person – on an unconscious, visceral level to understand and connect with another person. What brand strategists do is help translate that from individual to individual to your company. To help you develop a visceral-Companyence for the right people. You're not going to be the right practitioner for everyone, and you're not going to be the practitioner for most, but there are the right people, and for those right people, there will never be another practitioner who could replace you. Those are the people we need to make connections with, and yeah, some of it is the down-and-dirty bit, known as marketing and sales, that gets their attention, but it's the branding that keeps them.

I understand your frustration, and I have experienced it myself. However, I know that together, we can connect you with individuals who will not only benefit from your services but also value the contributions you can offer.

So now, my purpose is to connect you with the right people and clients so your frustration levels decline and your practice succeeds. I want your practice to become more profitable and fulfilling and for you to serve the patients you are meant to serve. And maybe, just maybe, people like my son won't get lost in the shuffle cause there will be more people like you, with the time, resources, energy, and skills who care.

Also by Alice Pettey:

Branding Your Practice takes the reader through the discovery of transformative strategies to elevate their health or wellness practice's branding. ***Branding Your Practice*** is not just a book; it's a step-by-step blueprint for cultivating a powerful brand identity.

Each section of the book takes the reader through a different section of the branding processes. Begining with understanding the the value of a brand, to learning about the elements that make up a brand and how they work together. Starting with Part Three the book takes on an interactive quality in working with the reader to directly create their branding from foundation, to internal compents and culture, through social and reputation management. The final section contains references and resources to support the reader through this proceess.

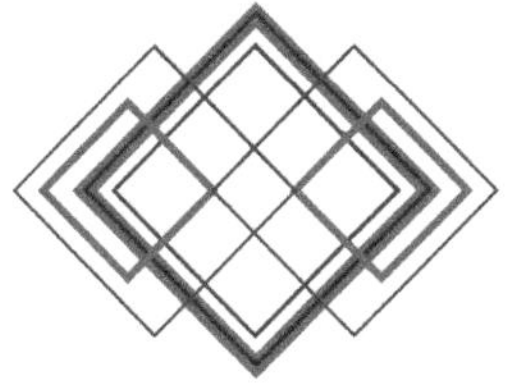

CHAPTER 12

Neurotic Dog Studios

At **Neurotic Dog Studios**, we know that branding isn't just about aesthetics—it's about making an impact. Your brand is the voice, identity, and trust signal that sets your health and wellness practice apart. Without a clear, compelling brand, you're leaving growth on the table. We specialize in transforming branding challenges into powerful opportunities that drive patient trust, engagement, and long-term success.

Who We Are

Neurotic Dog Studios was founded with a singular purpose: to help health and wellness providers build brands that not only stand out but truly connect. We're not just designers or strategists—we're brand architects who craft identities that inspire trust, loyalty, and credibility.

Our expertise goes beyond logos and color palettes. We create brands that **tell stories, cultivate meaningful relationships, and turn first-time patients into lifelong advocates**.

Why Health and Wellness?

In an industry built on trust and personal care, **your brand is**

everything. Patients need more than a service—they need confidence in their provider. Yet, many health and wellness practices struggle to convey their expertise, values, and unique approach.

That's where we come in. We help you:

✅ **Clarify Your Brand Message** – Eliminate confusion and clearly communicate why you are the best choice.✅ **Stand Out in a Crowded Market** – Attract the right patients by differentiating yourself with a brand that speaks to their needs.✅ **Build Trust and Loyalty** – A well-crafted brand fosters confidence, encourages referrals, and enhances patient retention.

What We Do

Our tailored branding solutions address every touchpoint of your practice's identity. Whether you need a complete rebrand or strategic refinements, we ensure your brand works for you—not against you.

Brand Strategy Development

We clarify your vision, mission, and values to create a **solid brand foundation** that guides all patient interactions and marketing efforts.

Visual Identity & Design

Your brand's first impression matters. We design logos, color palettes, and typography that reflect your expertise, professionalism, and unique approach to care.

Patient Experience Alignment

Branding isn't just external—it's felt at every touchpoint. We ensure your **in-office experience, website, and communication** align seamlessly with your brand message.

Marketing Collateral & Digital Presence

From brochures and social media graphics to website development, we create visually stunning and strategically powerful materials that attract, inform, and convert.

Why Choose Neurotic Dog Studios?

🔹 **Specialized in Health & Wellness:** We understand your industry's unique challenges and opportunities. 🔹 **Custom-Tailored Strategies:** Your practice isn't like any other—your branding shouldn't be either. 🔹 **Proven Track Record:** Our clients see measurable improvements in patient inquiries, retention, and overall practice growth. 🔹 **Full-Service Branding Partner:** We're with you every step of the way—from discovery to execution.

Your Next Step: Let's Build a Brand Patients Trust

You didn't start your practice to blend in—you started it to make a **difference**. Your brand should reflect that. **Now is the time to take control of your branding and position your practice for long-term success.**

📞 Schedule a Free Discovery Call Today

Let's talk about how we can **transform your branding** into one of your greatest business assets.

🔗 **Visit** neuroticdogstudios.com

📞 **Call Us:** 1.844.621.3433

📩 **Email:** info@neuroticdogstudios.com

🚀 **Your brand is your business's most valuable asset.**
Let's make it unforgettable.

Sechedule a
Free Discovery
call Today

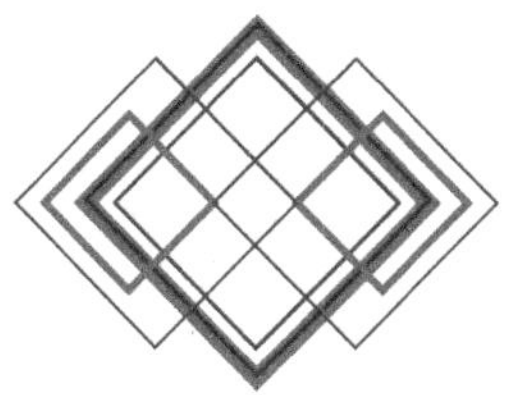

Bibliography

A

Accenture. (2021). *Why consumers pay more for trusted brands.* Retrieved from https://www.accenture.com

Accenture. *The role of branding in consumer decision-making.* Retrieved from https://www.accenture.com/branding-consumer-insights

Adobe. (n.d.). *The impact of design on consumer trust*. Retrieved from https://www.adobe.com

Adobe. *The importance of website design in building trust.* Retrieved from https://www.adobe.com/trust-building-design

B

BrandActive. (2023). *MedStar Health case study: Branding in healthcare.* Retrieved from https://brandactive.com/case-studies/branding-in-healthcare

BrightLocal. (2023). *Local consumer review survey 2023: How consumers use online reviews*. Retrieved from https://www.

brightlocal.com

BrightLocal. *The impact of online reviews on local businesses.* Retrieved from https://www.brightlocal.com/research

C

Covelli, A. F., & Barnes, H. (2023). *Novice nurse practitioners' employment decisions and role transition experiences during COVID-19.* Journal of Professional Nursing, 47, 81–87. https://doi.org/10.1016/j.profnurs.2023.05.009

E

Edelman. (2023). *2023 Edelman trust barometer.* Retrieved from https://www.edelman.com/trust/2023/trust-barometer

F

Forbes. (2018). *10 marketing, web design, and branding statistics to help you prioritize business growth initiatives.* Retrieved from https://www.forbes.com/sites/gabrielshaoo-lian/2018/08/10/10-marketing-web-design-branding-statistics-to-help-you-prioritize-business-growth-initiatives/

Forbes. (2020). *3 ways to build a consistent, polished, and engaging brand voice.* Retrieved from https://www.forbes.com/sites/rhettpower/2020/11/08/3-ways-to-build-a-consistent-polished-and-engaging-brand-voice/

Forbes. *How consistent branding can increase revenue by 23%.* Retrieved from https://www.forbes.com/sites/melissa-houston/2021/06/22/how-branding-can-10x-your-revenue-and-save-you-time

Forbes Business Development Council. (2023, February 15). *Brand consistency could be your biggest asset: 3 ways to make yours memorable.* Retrieved from https://www.

forbes.com/councils/forbesbusinessdevelopmentcouncil/2023/02/15/brand-consistency-could-be-your-biggest-asset-3-ways-to-make-yours-memorable/

Forrester. (2023). *The business impact of branding in health and wellness.* Retrieved from https://www.forrester.com

Frontify. *7 major benefits of a strong brand.* Retrieved from https://www.frontify.com/en/blog/7-major-benefits-of-a-strong-brand

G

Gallup. (2021). *State of the American workplace.* Retrieved from https://www.gallup.com

Gallup. (2023). *State of the global workplace report.* Retrieved from https://www.gallup.com

Glassdoor. (2023). *Employee engagement and workplace satisfaction survey.* Retrieved from https://www.glassdoor.com

Glassdoor. *Employee alignment and company success.* Retrieved from https://www.glassdoor.com/research

H

Harvard Business Review. (2022). *How strong brands build lasting patient loyalty.* Retrieved from https://hbr.org

Healthcare Success. *Building a trustworthy healthcare brand: Key strategies for growth.* Retrieved from https://www.healthcaresuccess.com

Hillen, M. A., Gutheil, C. M., Smets, E. M., & Han, P. K. (2021). *Patient perspectives on expectation communication and trust in healthcare: A qualitative study.* Journal of Patient Experience. National Library of Medicine. Retrieved from https://pmc.ncbi.nlm.nih.gov/articles/PMC7786689/

HubSpot. (n.d.). *The ultimate list of marketing statistics for 2024.* Retrieved from https://www.hubspot.com/marketing-statistics

I

Ignyte. (n.d.). *How a brand extension can help you capture market share.* Retrieved from https://www.ignytebrands.com/brand-extension/

J

Jadhav, M. S., & Bagul, D. B. (2023). *Healthcare branding and reputation management: Strategies for organizational success.* ResearchGate. Retrieved from https://www.researchgate.net/publication/378858532_Healthcare_Branding_and_Reputation_Management_Strategies_for_Organizational_Success

K

Kantar. (2022). *Brand equity and business performance in healthcare.* Retrieved from https://www.kantar.com

L

Lucidpress. (2022). *The ROI of brand consistency.* Retrieved from https://www.lucidpress.com

M

McKinsey & Company. (2022). *How healthcare branding impacts market growth.* Retrieved from https://www.mckinsey.com

N

Nielsen. (2023). *How brand storytelling drives engagement.* Retrieved from https://www.nielsen.com

P

PatientPop. (2023). *What patients expect from modern healthcare brands.* Retrieved from https://www.patientpop.com

PricewaterhouseCoopers (PwC). (2022). *The consumerization of healthcare: Building patient trust through branding*. Retrieved from https://www.pwc.com

W

Work Institute. (2021). *The cost of employee turnover in healthcare*. Retrieved from https://www.workinstitute.com

NeuroticDogStudios.com

Made in the USA
Las Vegas, NV
09 March 2025

19299037R00049